To:_____

From:_____

Date:_____

Together Is Forever

Scripture text taken from *The Holy Bible, New King James
Version*. Copyright © 1979, 1980, 1982 by Thomas Nelson, Inc.

Library of Congress Cataloging-in-Publication Data:
Together is forever.
p.   cm.
ISBN 0-8499-5160-7
1. Marriage—Religious aspects—Christianity. 2. Marriage—
Biblical teaching. 3. Love—Religious aspects—Christianity.
4. Love—Biblical teaching. I.Word Publishing.
BV4596.M3T64   1995
248.4—dc20
95-19169
CIP

Together Is Forever

WORD PUBLISHING
Dallas • London • Vancouver • Melbourne

*M*arriage is a dance of poetry.

Each lover bows to the other and says,

"No, please, you go first."

———

Let nothing be done through selfish ambition
or conceit, but in lowliness of mind let
each esteem others better than himself.

PHILIPPIANS 2:3

*A*ll the gold, silver, and platinum
in the world are not worth as much as the
abiding love you have for each other.

———◆———

Though you lie down among the sheepfolds,
you will be like the wings of a dove covered with
silver, and her feathers with yellow gold.

PSALM 68:13

$\mathcal{G}$od has reserved a cozy place

for you and your spouse in His heart.

When you are sad, give Him your every

burden. He will give you peace.

———◆———

God is love, and he who abides in love abides

in God, and God in him.

1 JOHN 4:16

$\mathcal{C}$ompassion, love, and courtesy:

these three legs of the relationship stool

will serve you well for a lifetime.

———◦———

Finally, all of you be of one mind, having
compassion for one another; love as brothers,
be tenderhearted, be courteous; . . .

1 PETER 3:8

$\mathcal{G}$od crowns each year of life

with His matchless love and goodness.

He prepares a way for you and the one

you love through all your days.

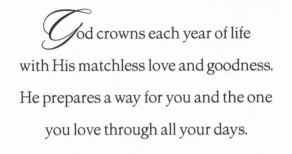

You crown the year with Your goodness, and Your
paths drip with abundance.

PSALM 65:11

$\mathcal{N}$ever tease or make light of

your spouse's most intimate thoughts or

desires. Help your beloved work out the

plan God has for his or her life.

———◦◦◦———

A friend loves at all times, and a brother is
born for adversity.

PROVERBS 17:17

$\mathscr{T}$rue love is a fortress against troubles

from all sides. It will help you withstand

the fierce storms and angry seas of

misunderstanding. Be strong together.

Though one may be overpowered by another,
two can withstand him.

ECCLESIATES 4:12

$\mathcal{I}$f you want your children to be

God-fearing men and women, you and

your mate must show them how

God-fearing people live.

———◆———

Blessed is the man who fears the LORD,
who delights greatly in His commandments. His
descendants will be mighty on earth; the generation
of the upright will be blessed.

PSALM 112:1, 2

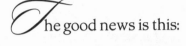

he good news is this:

You don't have to bear the challenges

of life alone. Speak the concerns of your

heart to your beloved. Then go together

to the Father in prayer.

Cast your burden on the LORD,
and He shall sustain you.

PSALM 55:22

$\mathscr{T}$roubles can steal the seeds of your

marital happiness before you even have

time to plant them. Ask God to help you

overcome your difficulties and challenges.

———◦◦◦———

The LORD your God, who goes before you,
He will fight for you.

DEUTERONOMY 1:30

*G*ive thanks to God and
to your spouse for the happiness you are
enjoying each day. Delight in the aware-
ness that *together is forever.*

———◆———

May my meditation be sweet to Him;
I will be glad in the LORD.

PSALM 104:34

*E*ven as you are drawn into a deeper relationship with your mate, a loving God seeks to draw you both closer to Himself.

———⊙———

But as for me, my prayer is to You, O LORD, in the acceptable time; O God, in the multitude of Your mercy, hear me in the truth of Your salvation.

PSALM 69:13

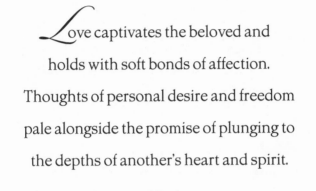

$\mathcal{L}$ove captivates the beloved and
holds with soft bonds of affection.
Thoughts of personal desire and freedom
pale alongside the promise of plunging to
the depths of another's heart and spirit.

I am my beloved's, and my beloved is mine.
SONG OF SOLOMON 6:3

$\mathcal{T}$he bonds of love that draw you to
each other are blessed by God. He wants
you to rejoice in these ties of love.

———◆———

God sets the solitary in families; He brings
out those who are bound into prosperity; but the
rebellious dwell in a dry land.

PSALM 68:6

$\mathcal{C}$an your beloved trust in
your fidelity and loyalty? Trust is a key
that keeps open the door of lifelong love
and mutual appreciation.

———❦———

The heart of her husband safely trusts her;
so he will have no lack of gain.

PROVERBS 31:11

$\mathcal{U}$se disagreements to build your

relationship. Talk about problems the

moment they occur. Don't let resentment

or anger build a wall between you

and the one you love.

———◉———

And if a house is divided against itself,
that house cannot stand.

MARK 3:25

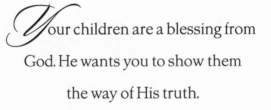

$\mathcal{Y}$our children are a blessing from

God. He wants you to show them

the way of His truth.

My son, hear the instruction of your father, and do
not forsake the law of your mother.

PROVERBS 1:8

*H*old your mate tightly when trouble

comes and begins to shake your lives. Let

tears bring healing to troubled waters.

—◦◦◦—

Blessed are those who mourn,
for they shall be comforted.

MATTHEW 5:4

*I*f you are impatient with God's work in your love relationship, don't hesitate to tell Him your concerns. Ask Him to make your love stronger each day.

It is time for You to act, O LORD, for they have regarded Your law as void.

PSALM 119:126

*T*he burdens of life may seem

impossible—but remember that

two people in love can pull a heavier load

together than each can pull alone.

———◈———

Two are better than one, because they have a good
reward for their labor.

ECCLESIASTES 4:9

$\mathcal{D}$elight in searching out the

hidden places of your beloved's mind

and soul. Give your heart to your love

and to none other.

———◦———

Drink water from your own cistern, and running
water from your own well.

PROVERBS 5:15

$\mathcal{R}$esentment slices through love. Its wounds can take a lifetime to heal. Give up your grudges. Tell your beloved how you feel and seek to live together in peace.

———◆———

The LORD will bless His people with peace.

PSALM 29:11

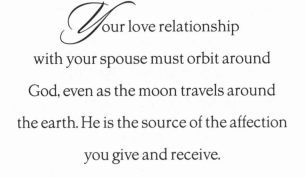

*Y*our love relationship

with your spouse must orbit around

God, even as the moon travels around

the earth. He is the source of the affection

you give and receive.

For You, O God, have tested us;
You have refined us as silver is refined.

PSALM 66:10

$\mathcal{G}$od has blessed you and

your beloved with His love and care.

He delights in pleasing you throughout all

your days.

———————

I will sing to the LORD, because
He has dealt bountifully with me.

PSALM 13:6

$\mathcal{L}$ift your eyes to the Lord of the Heavens and ask Him to shower your marriage with grace. He is the one who enables you to love.

———◦———

He shall come down like rain upon the grass before mowing, like showers that water the earth.

PSALM 72:6

$\mathcal{P}$rayer cements your heart to the heart of your beloved. Take time to pray with the one you love.

———◆———

For where two or three are gathered together in My name, I am there in the midst of them.

MATTHEW 18:20

$\mathcal{D}$on't withhold the sweetness of love from your spouse. Accept the delights of love with an open hand and give them freely to the one you love.

———◆———

My son, eat honey because it is good, and the honeycomb which is sweet to your taste.

PROVERBS 24:13

$\mathcal{V}$irtue is the foundation of a solid

marriage. Let your beloved know you will

be true in your affection. Don't squander

your love in unfaithfulness.

———◆———

Whoever commits adultery . . . lacks understanding;
he who does so destroys his own soul.

PROVERBS 6:32

*A*n affair begins with the eyes, so don't let your eyes deceive you. The one you desire might look attractive, but adultery ends in ugly arguments and tormented guilt.

———◈———

Better is the sight of the eyes than the wandering of desire. This also is vanity and grasping for the wind.

ECCLESIASTES 6:9

*L*ove is like a garden. The seed

of love is planted, but unless someone

tends the garden with tender, loving care,

a strong plant cannot grow.

———◆———

Let my beloved come to his garden and

eat its pleasant fruits.

SONG OF SOLOMON 4:16

$\mathcal{W}$ords can build a relationship or destroy it. Let your words be those that build honesty and love. Speak words of kindness and appreciation.

———◆———

Pleasant words are like a honeycomb. Sweetness to the soul and health to the bones.

PROVERBS 16:24

*M*ay your nights be filled with
the comfort of a binding love. Don't let the
distractions of the day intrude upon the
coziness of a night spent in the
arms of your beloved.

———◦◦◦———

Come, let us take our fill of love until morning;
let us delight ourselves with love.

PROVERBS 7:18

$\mathscr{S}$et your love with a seal—a seal that says our love is vital to our relationship. It will remind your beloved that you will be faithful and true, regardless.

———

Set me as a seal upon your heart, as a seal upon your arm; for love is as strong as death.

SONG OF SOLOMON 8:6

True love weathers every storm and outlasts every trouble. Let your love shelter the two of you forever.

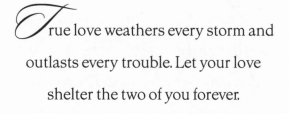

A man who has friends must himself be friendly, but there is a friend who sticks closer than a brother.

PROVERBS 18:24

*S*ometimes love is like awkward poetry.

The words may not be just right, but when

love comes freely from the heart,

the message sings.

———◦———

Many waters cannot quench love,
nor can the floods drown it.

SONG OF SOLOMON 8:7

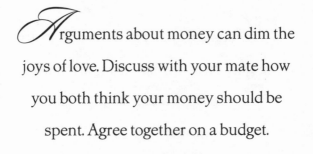

$\mathscr{A}$rguments about money can dim the joys of love. Discuss with your mate how you both think your money should be spent. Agree together on a budget.

———⊹———

Houses and riches are an inheritance from fathers,
but a prudent wife is from the LORD.

PROVERBS 19:14

$\mathcal{S}$eek harmony in your marriage.

Don't take detours to agreement.

Talk about your differences kindly and in

love until there is full understanding.

Be of good comfort, be of one mind, live in peace;
and the God of love and peace will be with you.

2 CORINTHIANS 13:11

*L*ove has a sweet savor. Enjoy the essence of the love you share with your beloved. Give yourselves perfumes and ointments that delight the senses.

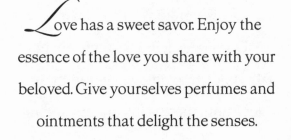

Ointment and perfume delight the heart . . .

<small>PROVERBS 27:9</small>

$\mathcal{M}$ake love to your spouse with abandon. Enjoy your nights together as much as you cherish your days.

Marriage is honorable among all,
and the bed undefiled.

HEBREWS 13:4

$\mathcal{P}$ut actions behind your words of love.

Don't just say "I love you"–

do something to bring a smile.

———◆———

My little children, let us not love in word or in

tongue, but in deed and in truth.

1 JOHN 3:18

$\mathcal{G}$od is the One who joined
you together. If you need guidance in
your marriage— and you will—ask the
One who ordained it.

For this reason a man shall leave his father and
mother and be joined to his wife, and the two shall
become one flesh. So then, they are no longer two
but one flesh. Therefore what God has joined
together, let not man separate.

MATTHEW 19:5–6

*B*e patient in your love. Do not
repeat harshness with harshness.
Give up the parting shot.

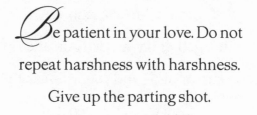

For if you love those who love you, what reward
have you? Do not even the tax collectors do the
same? Therefore you shall be perfect, just as your
Father in heaven is perfect.

Matthew 5:46, 48

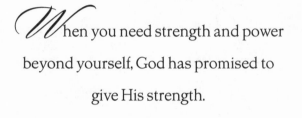

When you need strength and power
beyond yourself, God has promised to
give His strength.

Wait on the LORD; be of good courage, and He shall
strengthen your heart; wait, I say, on the LORD!

PSALM 27:14

$\mathcal{D}$evelop godly patterns in your marriage. Be kind, be patient, and pray to be filled with loving mercy.

———◆———

Therefore be merciful, just as your
Father also is merciful.

LUKE 6:36

$\mathcal{A}$re you overwhelmed by storms in your relationship? Don't despair. Ask God to bring His calm and abiding peace.

———•———

But He said to them, "Why are you fearful, O you of little faith?" Then He arose and rebuked the winds and the sea, and there was a great calm.

MATTHEW 8:26

$\mathcal{D}$o your actions match your words? Or do your words ring hollow and untrue. Be kind and considerate with the one you love.

———◦———

Though I speak with the tongues of men and of angels, but have not love, I have become sounding brass or a clanging cymbal.

1 CORINTHIANS 13:1

$\mathcal{C}$ling to the promises of God in the hard times. Talk to God about your deepest concerns—He has promised to listen.

———◈———

Blessed is the man who endures temptation;
for when he has been approved, he will receive the
crown of life which the Lord has promised
to those who love Him.

JAMES 1:12

*N*ever underestimate the power of love. The Bible tells us that love will always win the day!

———◆———

And now abide faith, hope, love, these three;
but the greatest of these is love.

1 CORINTHIANS 13:13

*H*ow special those times with
your mate that are filled with richness,
quietness, and contentment. Don't let
the endless pursuit of money or fame
substitute for tender times of nourishing
each other's spirits.

---

*Better a handful with quietness than both hands
full, together with toil and grasping for the wind.*

ECCLESIASTES 4:6

*C*hildren give you reasons to

reach beyond mediocrity. Let them inspire

you to do your best. Let them

prod you on to greatness.

———◈———

Like arrows in the hand of a warrior, so are the

children of one's youth. Happy is the man who

has his quiver full of them.

PSALM 127:4, 5

$\mathcal{L}$eave a legacy for your children.

Consider what you can do together to

make our planet a better place to live.

———◈———

One generation shall praise thy works to another,

and shall declare thy mighty acts.

$\mathcal{C}$omfort your beloved from a position of strength. Maintain courage, speak the truth in love, and comfort your spouse with words of encouragement.

———◦———

Therefore comfort each other and edify one another, just as you also are doing.

1 THESSALONIANS 5:11

$\mathcal{G}$od knows your concerns.

That's why He offers you a refuge

during life's storms.

———◆———

Trust in Him at all times, you people; pour out your

heart before Him; God is a refuge for us.

PSALM 62:8

$\mathcal{K}$eep your hopes high even when
your most cherished dreams seem
unattainable. Remember … with God
nothing is impossible.

*But Jesus looked at them and said, "With men
it is impossible, but not with God; for with God
all things are possible."*

MARK 10:27

$\mathcal{D}$on't focus conversation on your troubles. Remember, God loves a cheerful heart—and so does your spouse.

———

Anxiety in the heart of man causes depression, but a good word makes it glad.

PROVERBS 12:25

*W*hen you feel discouraged,

take comfort from past joys and successes.

Confidently plan your future

together—with God.

———

I remembered Your judgments of old, O LORD,
and have comforted myself.

PSALM 119:52

*H*onesty is vital to a loving relationship. If you are afraid of being open with your mate, practice being vulnerable before God. His boundless acceptance will give you courage.

———◆———

Search me, O God, and know my heart;
try me, and know my anxieties.

PSALM 139:23

When you feel hurt or unloved,
don't strike back. Revenge is no
building block for love.

*A soft answer turns away wrath,
but a harsh word stirs up anger.*

PROVERBS 15:1

*R*ead God's Word together every day.

As your souls grow closer to God, you

will grow closer to each other.

Have I not written to you excellent things of
counsels and knowledge, that I may make you
know the certainty of the words of truth?

PROVERBS 22:20–21

*R*ejoice in the pleasure God has given your marriage. Thank Him for the affection and passion you enjoy.

———◆———

They are abundantly satisfied with the fullness
of Your house, and You give them drink from
the river of Your pleasures.

PSALM 36:8

$\mathcal{F}$ocus on the positive things in your

marriage—those endearing qualities that

brought you and your mate together

in the first place.

For Your lovingkindness is before my eyes,
and I have walked in Your truth.

PSALM 26:3

The loyalty you feel for your beloved is precious beyond words. Stand beside your mate all the way—even in the hard times.

———

Entreat me not to leave you, or to turn back from following after you; for wherever you lodge, I will lodge; Your people shall be my people, and your God, my God.

RUTH 1:16

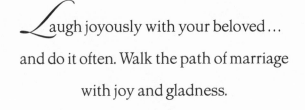

*L*augh joyously with your beloved ...
and do it often. Walk the path of marriage
with joy and gladness.

Light is sown for the righteous, and gladness
for the upright in heart.

PSALM 97:11

$\mathscr{S}$peak your emotions freely to your beloved. Your love will flourish with this outpouring of your heart.

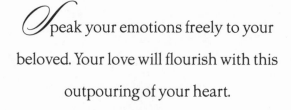

I cry out with my whole heart; hear me,
O LORD! I will keep Your statutes.

PSALM 119:145

$\mathcal{L}$ove your mate with the fruits
of the Spirit. Let your relationship be a
model for others to see—especially
your children.

*But the fruit of the Spirit is love, joy, peace,
longsuffering, kindness, goodness, faithfulness,
gentleness, self-control. Against such there is no law.*

GALATIANS 5:22, 23

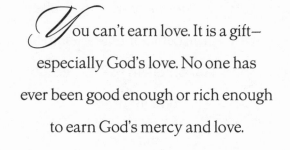

$\mathcal{Y}$ou can't earn love. It is a gift—
especially God's love. No one has
ever been good enough or rich enough
to earn God's mercy and love.

———◦———

He delivered me because He delighted in me.

PSALM 18:19

*I*f you have a love thought,

speak it now! There are no guarantees

for the days ahead.

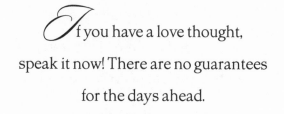

All flesh is as grass, and all the glory of man as the
flower of the grass. The grass withers and its flower
falls away, but the word of the Lord endures forever.

1 PETER 1:24, 25

$\mathcal{W}$e are all equally precious
in the eyes of the Father. Therefore, put
your beloved's concerns on an equal
footing with your own.

※

There is neither Jew nor Greek, there is neither
slave nor free, there is neither male nor female; for
you are all one in Christ Jesus.

GALATIANS 3:28

$\mathcal{C}$onceit is a dangerous ingredient

in love. You are walking on eggshells

when you think you have all the answers.

Look at both sides of the issue—it still

takes two to tango.

———◆———

Do you see a man wise in his own eyes? There is
more hope for a fool than for him.

PROVERBS 26:12

$\mathcal{L}$et your love blossom into a tree

that shades your lives with goodness

and contentment.

———◆———

Like an apple tree among the trees of the woods,

so is my beloved. . . .

SONG OF SOLOMON 2:3

*P*ray for your marriage with confidence. God cares about you and your beloved.

———◆———

For the eyes of the Lord are on the righteous,
and His ears are open to their prayers.

1 PETER 3:12

*E*ncourage your spouse with

reminders of what God has done for you.

Grow together in the knowledge of His

love and His goodness.

———◦◦◦———

But you, beloved, building yourselves up on your
most holy faith, praying in the Holy Spirit, keep
yourselves in the love of God, looking for the mercy
of our Lord Jesus Christ unto eternal life.

JUDE 20, 21

$\mathcal{C}$ount your blessings. Rejoice

in all that God has given to you and

your beloved.

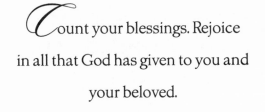

Come and see the works of God; He is awesome in
His doing toward the sons of men.

PSALM 68:5

*A*n enduring, loving marriage is a monument to the goodness of God. When gray hairs appear and bodies slow down, let your love for each other keep growing.

———◆———

Now also when I am old and grayheaded,
O God, do not forsake me, until I declare Your
strength to this generation, Your power to
everyone who is to come.

PSALM 71:18

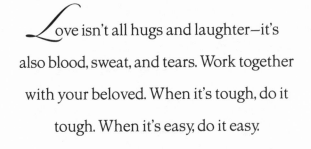

$\mathcal{L}$ove isn't all hugs and laughter—it's also blood, sweat, and tears. Work together with your beloved. When it's tough, do it tough. When it's easy, do it easy.

The soul of the diligent shall be made rich.

PROVERBS 13:4

$\mathcal{G}$od wants to bless you
and your loved one. Accept His love
and benediction.

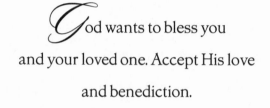

God be merciful unto us, and bless us;
and cause His face to shine upon us.

PSALM 67:1

$\mathcal{L}$ive so that you may look upon your work and pronounce it good. Let pride shine in your face when your labor is worthy of praise. Give glory to God for what you have accomplished.

———✦———

So I perceived that nothing is better than
that a man should rejoice in his own
works, for that is his heritage.

ECCLESIASTES 3:22

God's love wraps around
you and your beloved like a warm
blanket on a cold winter's night. His
love sustains a relationship that loves
to live and lives to love.

---

*O God, You have taught me from my youth; and to
this day I declare Your wondrous works.*

PSALM 71:17

TOGETHER IS FOREVER · 78

$\mathcal{L}$ove does not grow by ironclad rules, seeking to bend others to its own way. Love grows and flourishes in the gentle breeze of acceptance. Invite your mate into your heart with gentleness, not with legislation.

——◦——

Love does no harm to a neighbor; therefore love is the fulfillment of the law.

ROMANS 10:10

$\mathcal{M}$ake a daily decision to see the

workings of the Lord. See His hand in the

events that surround your marriage.

Thank Him for His constant, abiding help.

———◈———

I will also meditate on all Your work,
and talk of Your deeds.

PSALM 77:12

$\mathcal{T}$wo hearts don't always beat as one,

but in the important matters of life, seek

harmony with your mate.

———◆———

Again I say to you that if two of you agree on earth

concerning anything that they ask, it will be done

for them by My Father in heaven.

MATTHEW 18:19

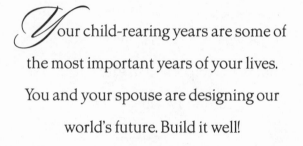

*Y*our child-rearing years are some of
the most important years of your lives.
You and your spouse are designing our
world's future. Build it well!

———————

Your seed I will establish forever, and build up
your throne to all generations.

PSALM 89:4

$\mathcal{L}$ie down in the warmth of God's love. He smiles when He sees the love between you and your mate in your most tender moments.

———◆———

For the LORD God is a sun and shield; the LORD will give grace and glory; no good thing will He withhold from those who walk uprightly.

PSALM 84:11

$\mathcal{G}$od has given you and your mate
different talents and abilities. Ask Him
how you can use your gifts to His glory.

———◦———

Your hands have made me and fashioned me;
give me understanding, that I may learn
Your commandments.

PSALM 119:73

*H*ow do you respond to the inadequacies you discover in yourself and your mate? Let God teach you to reflect His love and understanding.

———◦◉◦———

With all lowliness and gentleness, with longsuffering,
bearing with one another in love, . . .

EPHESIANS 4:2

$\mathcal{T}$he Bible gives a solid foundation for

relating justly and honestly to those

around you. Ask God for wisdom

as you work together to make

your marriage a success.

———◆———

Your word have I hidden in my heart,
that I might not sin against You.

PSALM 119:11

$\mathcal{L}$ove is a golden thread that,

when woven throughout your days,

makes your life a beautiful tapestry

for all to see.

Men shall speak of the might of Your awesome acts,
and I will declare Your greatness.

PSALM 145:6

*E*xercise caution in accepting financial counsel from those whose ethics may be in question. Choose your counselors and business associates with care. Your reputation, integrity, and honor are at stake.

———◆———

Blessed is the man who walks not in the counsel of the ungodly, . . . He shall be like a tree planted by the rivers of water, that brings forth its fruit in its season.

PSALM 1:1, 3

$\mathcal{L}$et your love be a hiding place for your beloved's imperfections. Praise your beloved. Let your pride in your loved one be seen by the glow on your face.

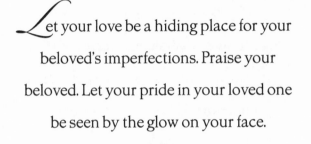

But above all these things put on love, which is the bond of perfection.

COLOSSIANS 3:14

*A*fter the sun has set and

darkness covers your face, seek the

sweet communion of time spent with

your beloved in the presence of God.

———◦———

I call to remembrance my song in the night;
I meditate within my heart, and my spirit
makes diligent search.

PSALM 77:6

*E*xplore the hidden beauties of your

spouse. Don't take your relationship for

granted. There is more to be discovered

than you will ever fathom.

———◦◉◦———

The LORD takes pleasure in those who fear Him,
in those who hope in His mercy.

PSALM 147:11

*Y*our words either build or destroy,

tear down or edify. Let loving speech—

coupled with loving actions—

be the proof of your love.

———

*Let your speech always be with grace, seasoned
with salt, that you may know how you ought
to answer each one.*

COLOSSIANS 4:6

$\mathcal{L}$oving criticism is better than lying praise. The one purifies so wounds can heal; the other encourages deceit to gain a temporary peace. Speak the truth in love.

———◆———

Faithful are the wounds of a friend, but the kisses of an enemy are deceitful.

PROVERBS 27:6

$\mathscr{P}$oliteness is grounded in truth and consideration. The roots of love grow deepest when truth is spoken in kindness.

———◈———

Keep your tongue from evil, and your lips from speaking deceit.

<small>PSALM 34:13</small>

$\mathcal{L}$ook at the face of your beloved and you will see flashes of gold—in fact, what you see is much more precious than gold.

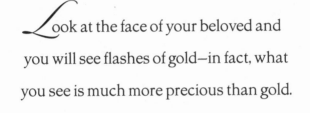

How fair and how pleasant you are, O love. . . .

SONG OF SOLOMON 7:6

A love that refuses to show its face is a worthless love. Never shy away from caring, honest reproof.

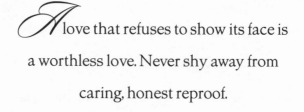

Open rebuke is better than love carefully concealed.

PROVERBS 27:5

$\mathcal{L}$ove is like an orchestra: The music and harmony of all the instruments *working together* creates a masterpiece.

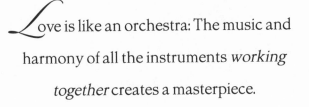

Love . . . does not behave rudely, does not seek its own, is not provoked, thinks no evil.

1 CORINTHIANS 13:4, 5

*W*hen you truly love, you ask, "What can I do for you?" not, " What have you done for me?"

———◆———

So husbands ought to love their own wives as their own bodies; he who loves his wife loves himself.

EPHESIANS 5:28

$\mathcal{G}$od has given you and your loved
one a bountiful marriage. Feast on the
delights of your love for each other.

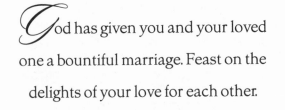

And they were both naked, the man and his wife,
and were not ashamed.

GENESIS 2:25

*G*od can make the rough ways

smooth and can heal your broken heart.

Rely on His grace to keep your marriage

healthy and strong.

———◦◦◦———

It is God who arms me with strength,
and makes my way perfect.

PSALM 18:32

*T*rue love is spun with the purest of

golden thoughts—enchanted dreams of

the next time you will be alone together.

———

So Jacob served seven years for Rachel,

and they seemed only a few days to him because

of the love he had for her.

GENESIS 29:20

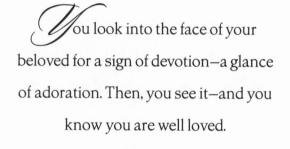

*Y*ou look into the face of your beloved for a sign of devotion—a glance of adoration. Then, you see it—and you know you are well loved.

My beloved is mine, and I am his.

Song of Solomon 2:16

*Y*our fears, joys, concerns, and moments of ecstasy are all part of the person God made you to be. Celebrate them *all* with your beloved.

From the end of the earth I will cry to You, when my heart is overwhelmed; lead me to the rock that is higher than I.

PSALM 61:2

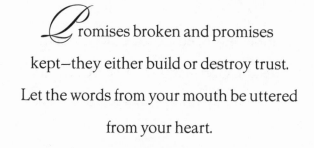

*P*romises broken and promises kept—they either build or destroy trust. Let the words from your mouth be uttered from your heart.

———◈———

A man's wisdom makes his face shine. . .

PSALM 61:5

$\mathcal{C}$omfort is the backbone of love.

Stand beside your beloved with

quiet encouragement.

———

I would comfort myself in sorrow;
my heart is faint in me.

JEREMIAH 8:18

$\mathscr{T}$rust is built when two people

keep and cherish each other's secrets.

Protect your beloved's privacy with the

same care you guard your own.

———

A talebearer reveals secrets, but he who is of

a faithful spirit conceals a matter.

PROVERBS 11:13

*T*rue love must stretch. Give your
beloved room to be the complete person
God has called him or her to be.

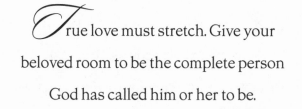

*For we through the Spirit eagerly wait for the hope of
righteousness by faith.*

GALATIANS 5:5

$\mathcal{I}$t is not useful to act as judge and jury

of your beloved's actions. Your task is to

love, listen, and care for the one you love.

————◆————

But God is the Judge; He puts down one,
and exalts another.

PSALM 75:7

*H*onest openness is the key to

being known by each other and feeling

the wondrous release of being truly

accepted by your beloved.

———◆———

Love . . . does not rejoice in iniquity, but
rejoices in the truth.

1 CORINTHIANS 13:4, 6

*K*indness must be woven

through the fabric of your love. This

thread must be strong enough to weather

the storms, and fragile enough to protect

the most gentle emotions.

———◦———

And be kind to one another, tenderhearted,
forgiving one another, even as God
in Christ forgave you.

EPHESIANS 4:32

$\mathcal{U}$nresolved anger opens wounds and causes pain. Cleanse your hurts before anger gains a foothold. Deal with the real issues—in truth and love.

He who gives a right answer kisses the lips.

$\mathcal{L}$ove can be clouded with discouragement, despair, and confusion. God promises to give you wisdom in all matters.

If any of you lacks wisdom, let him ask of God, who gives to all liberally and without reproach, and it will be given to him.

JAMES 1:5

*B*reathe deeply the fragrance of your love. Rejoice in the blessings you enjoy as a couple. Praise your heavenly Father for allowing you to be *forever in love*.

———◆———

Let your fountain be blessed, and rejoice with the wife of your youth.

PROVERBS 5:18

$\mathcal{L}$ove can strike like lightning—but
constant companionship and friendship
turn the first exhaustive moments of
passion into love for a lifetime.

*And may the Lord make you increase
and abound in love to one another and to all,
just as we do to you.*

1 THESSALONIANS 3:12

*I*n the soul of every man and woman is the desire to know God and to experience His divine love. Honor that desire in your mate—*together* make God the keystone of your marriage.

———◆———

Let all those who seek You rejoice and be glad in You; and let those who love Your salvation say continually, "Let God be magnified!"

PSALM 70:4

$\mathcal{S}$tamp CONFIDENTIAL across your marriage. The privacy you give each other frees you to share your innermost thoughts. Give this gift lavishly.

He who covers a transgression seeks love, but he who repeats a matter separates friends.

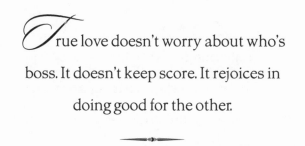

$\mathcal{T}$rue love doesn't worry about who's boss. It doesn't keep score. It rejoices in doing good for the other.

But he who is greatest among you
shall be your servant.

MATTHEW 23:11

$\mathcal{T}$rue love knits two people

together until the threads of one

life are intertwined inseparably

with those of the other.

———◦———

Behold, how good and how pleasant it is for

brethren to dwell together in unity!

PSALM 133:1

$\mathcal{E}$very romantic relationships falters at times. Often a wise, godly person can help when you do not know how to mend a broken relationship.

Where there is no counsel, the people fall; but in the multitude of counselors there is safety.

PROVERBS 11:14

*P*oets have tried for centuries to

capture the essence of love. God tells

us it is simply caring more about others

than about yourself. Love like

that is contagious!

———◆———

Nevertheless let each one of you in particular so love
his own wife as himself, and let the wife see that she
respects her husband.

EPHESIANS 5:33

$\mathcal{G}$entleness is the oil that smoothes

the friction of day-to-day living.

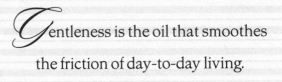

Let the husband render to his wife the affection due

her, and likewise also the wife to her husband.

1 CORINTHIANS 7:3

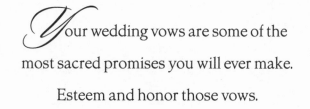

*Y*our wedding vows are some of the
most sacred promises you will ever make.

Esteem and honor those vows.

——

*For this reason a man shall leave his father
and mother and be joined to his wife, and the two
shall become one flesh.*

EPHESIANS 5:31

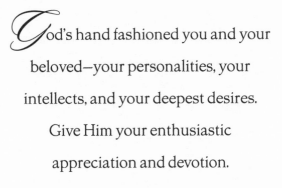

$\mathcal{G}$od's hand fashioned you and your

beloved—your personalities, your

intellects, and your deepest desires.

Give Him your enthusiastic

appreciation and devotion.

———◈———

LORD, You have been our dwelling place
in all generations.

PSALM 90:1

$\mathcal{R}$efresh yourself with the love
of your marriage. Let your affection for
one another be a soothing shade tree
during the dry and difficult
seasons of your lives.

*Walk in love, as Christ also has loved us
and given Himself for us.*

EPHESIANS 5:2

*H*old hands with your beloved.

Stand before God in gratitude for who He

is and what He has done in your lives.

———◈———

*I will praise You, O L*ORD*, with my whole heart;*
I will tell of all Your marvelous works.

PSALM 9:1

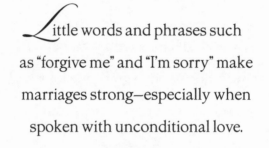

$\mathcal{L}$ittle words and phrases such as "forgive me" and "I'm sorry" make marriages strong—especially when spoken with unconditional love.

A word fitly spoken is like apples of gold in settings of silver.

PROVERBS 25:11

$\mathcal{D}$o not fear. God will shield you from all harm. Believe His promises and know that He will protect and guide you and the one you love.

———◆———

O God, behold our shield, and look upon the face of Your anointed.

PSALM 84:9

$\mathcal{C}$enter your heart around God and He will give you your desires. Come to God with your mate and dedicate your lives and your love to Him.

———❦———

Rejoice the soul of Your servant, for to You, O LORD, I lift up my soul.

PSALM 86:4

$\mathcal{L}$ove's first breath can be sweet, but

true love grows with the years until the

first blush becomes only a dim

shadow of the real thing.

———◦———

The end of a thing is better than its beginning; the
patient in spirit is better than the proud in spirit.

ECCLESIASTES 7:8

*Y*our conversation can be annoying—

like dripping water from a leaky faucet—

or it can gladden the heart like a

bubbling stream. It's *your* choice.

———◆———

If anyone does not stumble in word, he is a perfect
man, able also to bridle the whole body.

JAMES 3:2

*W*hen the challenges of life beat against you relentlessly, remember that God has promised to be your protection and your comfort.

The LORD is your keeper; the LORD is your shade at your right hand.

PSALM 121:5

God has made a commitment to you, your spouse, and your children. If you follow Him, He will remember you and redeem you.

———

He remembers His covenant forever, the word which He commanded, for a thousand generations.

PSALM 105:8

*W*hen the heartaches in life seem too much to bear, the heavenly Father will hide you under his powerful wings.

———

Keep me as the apple of Your eye; hide me under the shadow of Your wings.

PSALM 17:8

*I*f you and your mate cannot agree on which path to take, agree to disagree—but don't pull away from each other.

———◆———

Now the fruit of righteousness is sown in peace by those who make peace.

JAMES 3:18

$\mathscr{C}$elebrate every success with your mate. Enjoy the peaks of joy and happiness. Applaud your mate's achievements with enthusiasm.

———◦———

Let them do good, that they be rich in good works,
ready to give, willing to share.

1 TIMOTHY 6:17

$\mathcal{A}$sk God to keep your love alive.

He wants the best for the two of you as

you live and love together.

———◦———

And let the peace of God rule in your hearts, to
which also you were called in one body;
and be thankful.

COLOSSIANS 3:23

Other volumes to enjoy from the Moments for Your Life series include:

The Mirror Our Children See

God's Little Promise Book

God's Little Answer Book

God's Best for Your Success

Happiness Is…